CHRISTMAS Gifts, CHRISTMAS 'n Voices

JOHN ALLEN

Health Communications, Inc.
Deerfield Beach, Florida

www.hci-online.com

**Library of Congress Cataloging-in-Publication Data
is available from the Library of Congress**

©2002 John Allen
ISBN 0-7573-0053-7

Publisher: Health Communications, Inc.
3201 S.W. 15th Street
Deerfield Beach, FL 33442-8190

Cover and inside book design by Lawna Patterson Oldfield
Cover photo ©EyeWire Photography

This book is dedicated
to my mother,
who taught me
the true spirit of
Christmas.

Acknowledgments

First of all, I would like to thank Frank Weimann for having the vision to see this book's potential and Peter Vegso for the leadership to make it happen.

A special thanks goes to Christine Belleris, Allison Janse, Kathy Grant and the rest of the great staff at Health Communications, Inc., for their constant support.

I wish to express sincere appreciation to family, extended family and friends who have encouraged me on this project. There are certain individuals—you know who you are—who have gone above and beyond the call of duty in their support for this book. My brother and fellow writer, Sam, deserves special mention. (He is the author of one of the best series of woodworking books around, in my totally objective and unbiased opinion.)

And, of course, a heartfelt thanks goes out to my wife, JoAnn, for her role as editor/cheerleader/comforter/friend.

Chapter One

*I*t was a perfect life. And it was hard for Eric Sanders to imagine how things could be any better. He had a wonderful family, a comfortable house, a good job. He loved the small town where he lived. The pace of life was slower, the people were friendlier, and the sky was a clearer, purer blue.

Yes, it was a perfect life. And to make things even more perfect—it was Christmastime!

Eric's shoes crunched the crusted snow of the sidewalk as he walked along Main Street. He had taken part of the morning off to do some shopping. The cold temperature frosted his breath, making greetings to fellow towns-people visible as well as audible in the brisk air.

Eric undid the top button of his overcoat. He reached inside, probed a jacket pocket and pulled out a list he had made the night before while everyone was asleep. The list included the customary chocolates for business associates, the usual toys for some special nieces and nephews, a book for his brother, a fishing rod for his father and a sweater for his mother. But there were also some extra-special items on his list.

A new baseball glove for Billy. Eric thought back to a golden spring morning when Billy was seven. He found Billy sprawled out on the front porch, wholly absorbed in watching a potato bug meandering back and forth over the wooden planks.

"Billy."

No reply.

Eric repeated his name a little louder.

"Oh, hi, Dad. Potato bugs are neat. Did you know if you touch them they roll up and turn into BBs?"

"Yeah, they're pretty amazing aren't they. Hey, buddy, I've got something I want you to have." Eric held out a worn baseball glove. "This was mine. I know it doesn't look like much. But this is a magic glove. Really. You'll see. The trick is to not think of it as just a glove. When you put it on, let it become part of your hand, part of your body. And here's the magic part. Sometimes I'd be playing a game and a ball would come right out of nowhere. Before I'd even have time to think about it, my glove would pull my hand up to catch the ball."

"Is that really true, Dad?"

"Yeah, but before it can happen, you've really got to practice a lot."

For two years, Billy anxiously waited for the magic to happen.

"Why won't the glove work magic for me, Dad?"

"It will, son. But you've just got to keep practicing."

Then it finally happened. Eric had just returned from a seminar in Boston. Billy rushed up to him, sputtering, "Dad, Dad! It happened. The glove. It is magic."

"That's great, Billy. Let's go in and you can tell me all about it."

Billy proudly recounted how he had made a crucial catch, and how the glove had literally pulled his hand up to the ball. And he made a solemn vow to his dad. "Someday I'm going to play in the World Series!"

Eric smiled as he thought back to that special memory. For four years, the venerable glove had served Billy well. But now it was time to retire the battered old glove—to let Billy break in a new one and endow it with a special magic all its own.

A train set for Michelle. Not the usual gift for a

nine-year-old girl, but then Michelle wasn't your usual nine-year-old girl. She considered dolls for sissies. Last Christmas she got a junior carpenter's set. During the past year she had made a birdhouse, a doghouse (though they had no dog), a crooked bench and a crooked chair. And boxes. Boxes of all sizes. Boxes for toys, boxes for shoes and boxes for holding other boxes.

One chilly autumn day after work, Eric noticed Michelle leaning against the backyard fence. Something was different here. What struck Eric was that Michelle— usually busy building something, or climbing something or chasing something—was nearly motionless. As he approached her, he could see that she was looking past the large open field, intently staring off into the distance.

"What are you doing, Sis?"

"Just waiting for the train to come by . . ." She looked up at Eric. "Dad? Do you think I could ever build a train?"

"Michelle, you can do anything you put your mind to."

"Well, someday I'm going to build a train."

At least now you won't have to wait outside in the cold to see a train, Sis, thought Eric, as he continued down Main Street.

And an easel and art supplies for Leslie. She had often

told Eric about how she loved to paint back in high school. Eric had not known her then, but he had seen some of her paintings—paintings of mountains and horses and kittens and soft pastels of children.

"Why don't you take up painting again? You were really good," he once told her.

"Oh, I don't know. Maybe I'll surprise you and start painting again someday," she said.

"So why did you stop painting, anyway?"

"Oh, I don't know. I had big dreams. But I made the mistake of telling my mother about them. I told her that someday I was going to be a famous painter, and she laughed at me. Just her laughing at me was enough to make me lose interest in painting altogether."

I won't laugh at you, Les, thought Eric, as he crossed the street over to Mendelsohn's Hardware Store. Leslie had planned to meet Eric at Mendelsohn's to help with the shopping, but she woke up with a bad cold. "I'm determined to get better by Christmas," she said. "Why don't you go shopping yourself. I'll stay home and recuperate."

Mr. Mendelsohn normally only stocked the usual hammers and saws and screws and nails throughout the

year. But at Christmastime he always got in a big ship-
ment of toys and gift items.

As Eric surveyed a wall of toys, Mr. Mendelsohn came
up to him from behind. "May I help you, Mr. Sanders?"

"Oh, hi, Mr. Mendelsohn. I hope so. Do you have any
baseball gloves?"

"Baseball gloves I got. The ones I got left are kind of
large. But all you do is stuff a little tissue paper up into
the glove and it should fit just right for a boy. Here, what
do you think?"

Eric examined the glove. "There's just one thing," said
Eric, with a twinkle in his eye. "It has to be a magic
glove."

"A magic glove, you say. In that case, this—" he
handed Eric another identical glove "—is the glove you
want. One hundred percent guaranteed magic!"
Mendelsohn beamed.

"Great."

"Is there anything else you need?"

"Do you have any train sets?"

"Any particular scale?"

"Not really. Whatever you think a nine-year-old girl
would like."

"Probably the larger scale. I think I've got one in back. Let me go check; I'll be right back."

While he waited, Eric picked out some toys for his nieces and nephews. A few minutes later, Mendelsohn returned with a large box. "You're in luck, Mr. Sanders. This is my last train set."

"Great. I'll take it."

"Is there anything else?"

"You don't carry art supplies, do you?"

"No. For stuff like that you go to Kessler's—they usually stock art supplies."

On his way to Kessler's Office Equipment, Eric bought a fishing pole at Sommerby's Sports and chocolates at Mrs. Tate's Homemade Candies. Eric looked at his watch. The morning was nearly half gone. He decided he'd have to get his brother's book and his mother's sweater tomorrow.

From the street, Eric could see Mr. Kessler in the storefront window working on a Christmas display.

"I'm no good at this," complained Kessler as Eric entered the store. A couple of green plastic garlands entwined Kessler's arms and legs like a pair of benign boa constrictors. "Mrs. Kessler's the one who usually does this, but she's down with the flu."

"Yeah, my wife's sick, too, with a cold. And three people in our office are out sick."

"There's always a lot of illness this time of year. Well, let me know if there's any way I can help you."

"Actually, I wanted to look at your art supplies."

Kessler looked happy for an excuse to disentangle himself from the garlands. He led Eric to a corner of the store and helped him pick out paints, brushes and a palette.

"Will that do it for you, Mr. Sanders?"

"Do you have any easels?"

"Sure. Taking up painting are you, Mr. Sanders?"

"No, it's for my wife."

"Let's see what you think about this." Mr. Kessler set up an easel.

Eric gripped it near the top. It wobbled. He noticed the easel was made of particle board.

"Hot dog wood"—that's what Leslie would call it. When they were first married, Eric bought an inexpensive bookcase. The bookcase displayed in the store looked fine. But they were sold unassembled, and as Eric laid out the pieces on the front room floor, parts of the bookcase, hidden when put together, were exposed. You could see that beneath the thin wood-finish veneer, the bookcase was actually made of cheap particle board. When Leslie entered the room, she said, teasingly, "So you got us a bookcase made of hot dog wood."

"Hot dog wood?" said Eric, bewildered.

Leslie ran a finger across the lumpy edge of a section of particle board. "Yeah, hot dog wood. Because you really don't know what's in it, do you?"

Eric shifted his focus from the easel to Mr. Kessler and asked, "Do you have any other easels?"

"There's this. It's more expensive, but it's a lot nicer."

The easel was made of solid oak. Mr. Kessler set it up. Eric tested it to see if it wobbled. It didn't. "I'll take this, Mr. Kessler."

The easel barely fit into Eric's already crowded car trunk. He looked at his watch. 11:45. He decided to go back to the office for a half hour to organize his afternoon and then go home for a quick lunch.

Chapter Two

*E*ric opened the front door and paused in the living room to look at the Christmas tree. There was already a colorful pile of gifts from friends and relatives forming around the base of the tree. The packages were metallic green and crimson and gold and silver. And the shimmering brightness of the packages seemed to force the tree itself to compete for attention.

Eric found Leslie in her robe talking on the hall phone.

"Okay . . . We'll be there then . . . all right . . . Okay. See ya." Leslie put down the phone.

Eric kissed her and asked, "Who was that?"

Leslie pulled a face. "Oh, it was Janice Thompson. Apparently she remembers me promising I'd sing in the Christmas program. And she wants the children to sing in the children's choir."

"You told her you were sick, didn't you?"

"Yes, but you know how she is. She won't take no for

an answer. And the woman is shrewd. She appeals to your ego. 'You and your lovely children sang so wonderfully in last year's program that we simply couldn't dream of putting it on without you this year.' It was the part about the 'lovely children' that got to me. Anyway, she wants me and the kids to come to a practice tonight. She said it would just be a short practice and that getting a little fresh air would probably do me good. Like I said, the woman won't take no for an answer."

"Well, that certainly sounds like Janice, all right." Then Eric added, as one conspirator to another, "You know, if you want, I could call her later and tell her that I forbid you to leave your sick bed."

"I might just take you up on your offer. Come on in the kitchen. I made some hot soup."

Eric sat at the table.

"I got a lot of shopping done this morning," he said.

"What did you get?"

"I got Michelle a train set, and a baseball glove for Billy, and something for you."

"Something for me?" she said brightly, launching into what had become an annual routine for them. "Is it edible?"

"No comment."

"Is it something you wear?"

"No comment."

"Just tell me, how big is it? Can you hold it in your hand?" She suddenly smiled mischievously. "Or wear it on your hand?" she asked, waving a hand with fingers outspread.

"Look, all I'll say is this: It's edible, it's also flammable, and it glows in the dark."

"Oh, you didn't!" she exclaimed with mock excitement. "Are you saying you got me my favorites? Flaming, phosphorescent chocolate-covered cherries!"

"Oh, good guess, Les, but you're *way* off," Eric deadpanned.

Chapter Three

*A*s it turned out, Leslie and the kids went to the choir practice. After dinner, Eric remembered the gifts in the trunk, and while everyone was busy getting ready for the practice—brushing hair, washing faces and changing clothes—Eric stealthily maneuvered the gifts up to the attic. The attic, during Christmastime, was sacrosanct. Those in the family who were under thirty or female were forbidden to enter it. A somewhat similar rule applied to the basement, prohibiting entrance to family members under thirty or male.

Eric sat cross-legged in the middle of the attic floor. The baseball glove and the train set had been easy to wrap. But he knew the easel was going to be a challenge. He looked at his watch. If Janice Thompson was true to her word, the practice should be ending right about now.

He regarded the easel and realized that he was going to need more wrapping paper. He stood up and stretched, went downstairs to the closet where they kept the wrapping paper and selected an unused roll. Back in the attic, Eric faced the easel, determined to do a first-rate job of wrapping it. Soon after he began, however, he realized that he was going to have to settle for a less-than-perfect job. He looked at what he had done so far and winced: the paper was loose-fitting with awkward folds. *Okay, so it doesn't have to be beautiful, just as long as it's functional,* mused Eric, as he continued his functional if not beautiful job of wrapping the easel.

He heard a distant siren. The sound was both urgent and plaintive. While the sound of sirens always disturbed Eric, he found them especially troubling at Christmas: blaring intrusions that shattered his fragile ideal of a season filled with nothing but peace and happiness and joy.

As he continued working on the easel, Eric had to disregard every rule of gift wrapping he had ever learned. He finally decided to wrap it Egyptian mummy style and simply unwound the roll round and round until the easel was fully covered. The paper puckered and crinkled in several spots. But this only made it harder to discern what was beneath the paper. If Eric had to guess, he would probably say the gift was a large stuffed giraffe.

Eric was tying a bow on the oddly shaped bulk when he heard a faint rapping sound. Could it be someone at the front door, Eric wondered, or was it just another one of those phantom household sounds—unexplainable and presumably without significance? Since he couldn't be sure, he decided he'd better go down and find out. As he started down the stairs he heard a definite knocking sound again—only louder. Bounding down the steps, he called out, "Coming" in sing-song fashion. When he opened the door, he was surprised to find a large policeman standing on the porch.

"Mr. Sanders?"

"Yes . . ."

"I'm afraid I've got some bad news for you. There's been an accident . . ."

Eric's body froze. "Was anyone hurt badly?"

"Mr. Sanders," the officer's voice broke, "I am so sorry. . . ."

READER/CUSTOMER CARE SURVEY

BB1

We care about your opinions. Please take a moment to fill out this Reader Survey card and mail it back to us.
As a special **"thank you"** we'll send you exciting news about interesting books and a valuable **Gift Certificate.**

Please PRINT using ALL CAPS

First Name |_____| MI. |__| Last Name |_____|

Address |_____|

City |_____| ST |__| Zip |__|__|__|__|__| — |__|__|__|__|

Phone # (|__|__|__|) |__|__|__| — |__|__|__|__| Fax # (|__|__|__|) |__|__|__| — |__|__|__|__|

Email |_____|

(1) Gender:
____ Female   ____ Male

(2) Age:
____ 12 or under   ____ 40-59
____ 13-19   ____ 60+
____ 20-39

(3) Marital Status
____ Married
____ Single
____ Divorced/Widowed

(4) Did you receive this book as a gift?
____ Yes   ____ No

(5) How many Health Communications books have you bought or read?
____ 1   ____ 2-4   ____ 5+

(6) How did you find out about this book?
Please fill in ONE.
1) ____ Recommendation
2) ____ Store Display
3) ____ Bestseller List
4) ____ Online
5) ____ Advertisement
6) ____ Catalog/Mailing
7) ____ Interview/Review (TV, Radio, Print)

(7) Where do you usually buy books?
Please fill in your top TWO choices.
1) ____ Bookstore
2) ____ Religious Bookstore
3) ____ Online
4) ____ Book Club/Mail Order
5) ____ Price Club (Costco, Sam's Club, etc.)
6) ____ Retail Store (Target, Wal-Mart, etc.)

(9) What subjects do you enjoy reading about most? Rank only **FIVE**. Use 1 for your favorite, 2 for second favorite, etc.

	1	2	3	4	5
1) Parenting/Family	○	○	○	○	○
2) Relationships	○	○	○	○	○
3) Recovery/Addictions	○	○	○	○	○
4) Health/Nutrition	○	○	○	○	○
5) Christianity	○	○	○	○	○
6) Spirituality/Inspiration	○	○	○	○	○
7) Business Self-Help	○	○	○	○	○
8) Teen Issues	○	○	○	○	○
9) Sports	○	○	○	○	○

(14) What attracts you most to a book?
(Please rank 1-4 in order of preference.)

	1	2	3	4
1) Title	○	○	○	○
2) Cover Design	○	○	○	○
3) Author	○	○	○	○
4) Content	○	○	○	○

TAPE IN MIDDLE; DO NOT STAPLE

BUSINESS REPLY MAIL
FIRST-CLASS MAIL PERMIT NO 45 DEERFIELD BEACH, FL

POSTAGE WILL BE PAID BY ADDRESSEE

HEALTH COMMUNICATIONS, INC.
3201 SW 15TH STREET
DEERFIELD BEACH FL 33442-9875

FOLD HERE

Comments:

Chapter Four

*T*here was a great outpouring of love: food, cards, flowers and hugs. Everything he had ever felt about the town and its people was confirmed. Decent, concerned, caring—these were the words that came to mind.

In theory, Eric was in charge of making the arrangements. But in actuality, he simply allowed the tide of activity surrounding him to pull him along. He listened to people talk while he merely nodded his head or grunted. He felt numb, as people swirling around him spoke of caskets, burial plots, burial clothes and the funeral program.

Day and night became one. Short, fitful naps punctuated a dream-like existence of wandering aimlessly from one room to the next, doing mundane tasks like shaving and eating, and being asked to make decisions that had a context he couldn't comprehend.

One of the speakers at the funeral talked about triumph out of tragedy. The words sounded hollow and phony as Eric stared in disbelief at the three caskets before him.

"Let Dad and I stay with you for a while, or come stay with us," Eric's mother had offered. But somehow he felt more comfortable being alone.

For several days after the funeral, Eric went through cycles of denial, then bitter acceptance, bursts of anger ending in tears and sobbing, then denial all over again.

Whenever he looked at the brightly wrapped gifts surrounding the Christmas tree, he actually felt physical pain: a tightening in his chest and throat.

He finally called a local charity and told the woman on the phone that he had some Christmas gifts he wanted to donate.

"I'll be making some pick-ups this afternoon," she said. "Will you be home?"

"Yes."

"Well, if you'll just give me your address, we'll be by sometime between 2:30 and 4:00."

The woman showed up around 3:30 with a teenage boy. "You can take all those things under the tree," Eric said, waving a hand towards the pile.

"All of them?" said the boy, wide-eyed.

The woman shot the boy a guarded look. The look said, *If the man wants to give us a whole pile of wrapped gifts, act natural and don't ask questions.* . . .

"Yeah, they're all for you," Eric replied. "Here, let me help you."

For the next ten minutes, they loaded the gaily colored boxes into an old battered pickup. The pickup was a ridiculous shade of baby blue, accented with gray splotches of primer. About midway through the packing process, Eric noticed a change in the woman's eyes. They took on a knowing look, a look of pity. It was clear that she had finally connected Eric with the recent tragedy. But the boy's eyes remained uncomprehending.

Eric insisted they also take the Christmas tree—decorations and all.

"You moving or something, mister?" asked the woman's bewildered helper. The woman gave the boy another hard look, sharper than the first.

"I'm not celebrating Christmas this year," Eric said quietly.

"You have to excuse the boy for being so inquisitive, Mr. Sanders. But we surely do thank you for your generosity," said the woman, then added automatically: "Merry Christmas." Almost immediately, she knew her words were inappropriate. She was flustered and trying hard to hide it, which resulted in emphasizing her discomfiture.

Eric stood in his front yard and watched the ancient pickup sputter down the street. Although he wasn't dressed for the cold air, Eric lingered a few moments outside. He listened to some dogs barking playfully and to the sound of distant children's laughter, then reluctantly went back into his quiet house.

Chapter Five

*D*uring the next few days, friends and neighbors continued stopping by to express sympathy. They presented Eric with baked goods, inspirational books and heartfelt hugs. One afternoon, as Eric sat in his favorite overstuffed chair in the living room, he remained virtually motionless for several hours. He indulged in something he had been afraid to do since the accident. He indulged in pure nostalgia. He recalled bits of conversation, images and situations, all relating to his family.

In his mind, he saw Michelle at four dressed up in Leslie's clothes, wearing heels and walking with the trepidation of one trying stilts for the first time.

He saw Billy's hapless, dejected look upon being ordered to return a stolen candy bar to Swenson's Drug Store.

He recalled when Michelle was first learning to talk. Leslie would say, "Michelle, I love you very much," to which Michelle invariably replied in a spirit of one-upmanship, "I love you much-er."

He thought of other things Billy and Michelle had said using the logical but incorrect grammar of children. Anything better than "good" was, of course, "gooder." And if the past tense for "walk" was "walked," surely the past tense for "hurt" was "hurted." And Eric could still hear Michelle yelling with accusatory outrage: "Billy hitted me!"

He remembered coming home after work and seeing Leslie, exhausted from a full day of painting the kitchen and sewing room, wearing old work clothes and covered with splotches of peach and maroon, yet looking beautiful as ever.

He remembered attending a college dance. He couldn't remember who his date was for the night; all he could remember was noticing a lovely young woman with strawberry blonde hair and an infectious smile—and his total inability to refrain from staring at her throughout the evening.

On their first date, everything went wrong. His car broke down. They abandoned the car and took a taxi. They arrived at the theater ten minutes late. The usher refused to seat them because the play was already in progress. "You can take your seats during the intermission," she said. "In the meantime, you can watch the play on one of our lobby TV monitors." *Oh, great,* thought Eric. *Here I promised her a rich theatrical experience, and here we are standing in the lobby watching a small television screen.*

Later that evening, when Eric received the check for dinner, he experienced a horror he had only seen portrayed in television sitcoms: He didn't have enough money to pay for dinner. Somehow Leslie sensed Eric's predicament, made a joke of it, and—despite Eric's protests—gave him enough money to pay the bill.

That night, Eric lay awake in bed reconciled that he would never have another date with Leslie. Two weeks later, in a state of utter despair and feeling like a soldier on a suicide mission, Eric called Leslie. He knew she would say no to a date, but for some crazy reason he wanted a sense of closure concerning the girl with the strawberry blonde hair and the infectious smile. Somehow, a tangible, definite ending would help him move on with his life. After Leslie said hello, he muttered something about going out for pizza. "Sure," said

Leslie. "I was beginning to wonder why you hadn't called."

That was Leslie for you, thought Eric. The only predictable thing about Leslie was that she was unpredictable. Eric looked across the living room at her picture on the piano. The sun was beginning to set, and in the dimness he could barely make out her features. He finally closed his eyes and clearly saw her face. She could forgive the unforgivable, make a joke out of a disaster, show strength that belied her carefree manner, and yet at times burst into tears without warning.

Eric remembered how she had worried about renewing her driver's license.

"This time, besides the written test, I'm going to have to actually drive," Leslie complained. "And you know me, Eric. I've never learned to parallel park, and I can't remember if you're supposed to look in the rearview mirror every ten seconds or every five seconds."

"You're a good driver, Les. You've got nothing to worry about."

"Could I ask you a favor? Would you come with me for moral support?"

"Sure."

The night before her test, Eric somehow sensed he was alone in bed and half woke up from a deep sleep. He heard some vague rattling noises from downstairs. *Poor kid,* he thought. *She's really nervous.* But since he couldn't think of anything to say to comfort her, he rolled over and went back to sleep.

In the morning, Leslie seemed surprisingly calm and cheerful. "You know, Eric, you really don't have to come with me this morning. I'll be fine."

"It's okay. I'll come, Leslie. I've already taken the morning off."

They had to go to Sommerville for the test. Eric waited in a spartan foyer for Leslie. After an hour, Leslie returned from her ordeal all smiles.

On the way home, Eric said, "Okay, Leslie, come clean. You've been a bundle of nerves the past couple of weeks. And yet today you're cool as the proverbial cucumber. What gives?"

"Okay. It's like this, I got this idea last night. For some reason, I remembered this story I heard when I was a kid in Sunday school. You see, there's this guy—I don't remember his name—and he's the eldest, so he's got the birthright—I guess that means he inherits everything.

Well anyway, he's walking along, and he smells some pottage. And his brother's cooking it. Well, the pottage smells so good—I can't imagine anything called 'pottage' smelling good—but it smells so good, he sells the brother his birthright for the pottage.

"No offense," Leslie grinned, "but men are funny creatures. And I got to thinking, if a guy would sell his birthright for some smelly old pottage, what would he do for a smooth piece of fudge—fudge with marshmallow topping!

"Well, last night I stayed up and made a batch of fudge. Here, have some."

The creamy, buttery square melted in his mouth.

"Before we got started on the driving part of the test," continued Leslie, "I gave the officer two pieces of fudge.

"I'm sure I made a lot of mistakes, but the officer was too busy eating the fudge to notice."

"You know," said Eric, "you would have made a pretty good spy: passing out fudge and getting everyone to divulge state secrets." He licked some fudge from the corners of his mouth. "Great fudge, by the way."

They stopped at an intersection. "So let's see your picture, Les."

"Oh, it's lovely—squinty eyes and all." She handed him the license.

Beyond the half-shut eyes, the picture conveyed the sense of relief Leslie was feeling that moment for passing the test.

Above the picture, Eric noticed a red square with white block letters: DONOR.

"So what's this?" he asked, indicating the red square as he handed the card back to Leslie.

"No big deal. It just means that I'm an organ and tissue donor. They asked me about it, and I said sure. They told me a little about it—and it's really amazing what parts of the body can be reused to help others."

"Wait a minute, Leslie," Eric tried to control his exasperation at Leslie's casual tone. "You're not planning on going anywhere, are you?"

Leslie was suddenly very serious. "No. But that's just it. Nobody does."

🍂

In the dark stillness, Eric heard the mournful sound of a distant train whistle. He thought of Michelle waiting to see the train on that chilly afternoon. He instantly re-membered the train he had bought for her.

And in a sudden rush of comprehension, he realized that all the gifts he had wrapped in the attic were still there. The easel and art supplies, the baseball glove, the train set.

Was it too late to call the lady from the charity? Eric thought for a moment and decided that tonight was quite possibly Christmas Eve. He went to the kitchen calendar and confirmed his suspicion.

He poured himself a glass of milk and sat at the kitchen table. It would be a shame to just let the gifts remain in the attic. Eric resolved that tonight he would play Santa Claus and deliver the gifts himself. *Leslie would like that,* he thought.

Now the only problem was to decide who should receive the gifts. First of all, the baseball glove. He remembered that Billy's friend Donny Shumway loved baseball. But he also remembered that Donny's parents gave him everything. He probably already had the finest baseball glove money could buy.

Who was that other boy Billy played with? Chet . . . that was it, Chet Anderson. A year ago, Eric thought he'd heard something about Chet's father having lost his job. Chet always wore old hand-me-downs. His sad countenance suggested that he carried burdens no child should be expected to bear. One day Chet was at the house playing with Billy, and Eric offered each boy an apple. He remembered that while Billy was still chewing on his second bite, Chet was wiping his mouth and asking where to put the core. From then on, whenever Chet was at the house, Eric always made a point of offering the boys treats—and he made sure that Chet got seconds.

Even though Eric wasn't sure if Chet liked baseball or not, he decided that he would give him the glove.

Now the train set. He mentally went down the list of Michelle's friends and couldn't think of one who would like a train set. Dolls, yes. Stuffed animals, yes. But train sets, no. There had to be someone who would like a train. For some reason, Eric thought about the couple who cleaned the office at night. Why would he think of them? Then he remembered: They had a son. He had met their son once or twice when he had been at the office working late. He was a nice, well-mannered boy. And he deserved a train for Christmas. After some thought, Eric recalled the name of the family. He got a phone book and wrote down their address.

Now for the easel and art supplies. This would be hard. Eric would have to think of someone a little older. He thought of some of the older kids and teenagers he knew, but none of them were really interested in art. Yes, this was going to be hard. Eric got another glass of milk.

When the glass was two thirds empty, it came to him. *Of course.* Their occasional babysitter, Ellen Michelsen.

He remembered coming home after a dinner out with Leslie and finding Ellen on the couch huddled over a sketchpad. Eric and Leslie stood behind the couch and watched her draw. She was working on a landscape featuring a large wheat field in the background and a dilapidated barn in the foreground. Leslie finally broke the silence. "That's really nice."

"*Oh!* Mrs. Sanders! You startled me," said Ellen and continued rapidly. "I didn't hear you come in. It's just that the children went to bed about a half an hour ago. They were good as usual, but I'd been playing with them the whole night, and this was my first chance to have any time to myself. I just don't want you to think I've been sitting here drawing all night."

"That's fine, Ellen," said Leslie. "But I must say, you're really talented. How long have you been drawing?"

"I guess most of my life. I really love it."

"Well, let me give you some advice, Ellen: Don't ever stop." Leslie looked wistful for a moment, then added, "You've got too much talent to ever let it go to waste. . . ."

🎄

Eric had an uncanny feeling as he entered the attic and saw the gifts just as he had left them. Everything suddenly seemed too unreal to fathom. Was everything just a dream? Had his life become a bad dream? But as he picked up the gifts, they felt real enough. And these tangible gifts that had weight and dimension dashed his fleeting, fantastic notion that all he had to do was wake up to make things normal again.

🎄

This must be how a burglar feels, thought Eric, as he cautiously approached the Anderson's small house. He'd parked half a block down the street. Even though he had made a point of wearing a dark jacket and slacks, he still felt very conspicuous. And although it was nighttime, his dark clothes were still quite noticeable contrasted against the white snow. *Just pretend you're out for an evening stroll,* he thought, clutching the glove. As he opened the old wooden gate, the rusted hinges made a shrill grating noise that shattered the evening silence. Eric sprinted to the doorstep, dropped the glove, and ran to the street, not bothering to close the annoying gate.

Just pretend you're out for an evening jog, he told himself as he ran to his car.

There was no noisy gate to contend with at the next house and he delivered the train set without incident.

Now for the easel, thought Eric, as he drove to Ellen's house.

When he entered the yard, a dog began barking. He remembered the Michelsen's had a large, aggressive dog named Barnaby. *Surely they keep him fenced at night,* thought Eric, hopefully. During the day, Barnaby roamed the neighborhood, glad for any leftovers that might be offered him. And because most folks were intimidated by the fierce-looking dog, they usually gave him generous helpings of old meat and bones and decaying casseroles in hopes of keeping him appeased. Eric remembered Leslie joking about the dog's name. "Barnaby?" she said. "That's too gentle-sounding. *Brutus*—now there's a name that fits him."

The barking became louder, and Eric watched in horror as Barnaby rounded a corner of the house and bounded straight for him. The dog pounced, knocking Eric down. Eric could see the hot breath coming from the dog's mouth. Remarkably, the dog suddenly stopped barking. Panting in an exhausted but friendly manner, the dog stepped off Eric and sat scrutinizing him. *He must recognize me as one of his faithful feeders,* thought Eric, gratefully.

As he stiffly got up from the ground, Eric noticed the easel laying in the snow. There was a large, open gash in the wrapping paper. *Oh well,* he thought as he removed and crumpled the paper, finding the easel still intact, *it's probably for the best: it was a lousy wrapping job, anyway . . .*

He left the easel set up on the porch with Barnaby faithfully guarding it.

WILDERMUTH

Chapter Six

*T*he passing of Christmas didn't diminish Eric's grief. Everything reminded him of his family. On his way to the store, he'd pass the ballfield where Billy used to play. At the store, he'd see a friend of Michelle's. And he always had to take a longer, roundabout route home so as to avoid the intersection where the accident had occurred.

It was mid-January. It had been tentatively decided that Eric would not return to work until February. He hadn't objected when his boss suggested he take a leave of absence. *But what magical thing is going to happen in February to make everything all right?* reflected Eric, bitterly.

One night, with a radio on in the kitchen and the television on in the front room, Eric restlessly walked from one room to the next. (He seldom paid attention to the TV or radio; he simply used them as a means of eliminating silence.)

He decided to clean his desk and get rid of unnecessary papers. He found an agenda for a seminar he'd attended years ago. *Guess I don't need this,* he thought, as he added it to the pile of papers to be discarded. Somehow his eyes focused on a name on the agenda. One of the speakers was Frank Smith. He'd first met Smith at a seminar in Boston several years ago, and over the years they continued to encounter each other at seminars and conventions. Eric suddenly remembered a conversation he'd had some years ago with Smith.

During a particular seminar, Smith took Eric to dinner. Smith introduced him to pheasant and other delicacies. During the dessert, whose roaring flames had just been extinguished, Smith asked with contrived casualness, "Eric, why are you wasting your talent out there in the hinterlands? Tell you what. You come work for me. You'll make three, four times what you're making there. And the projects we work on are really big. A guy like you needs a challenge. Well, we'll give you all the challenge you'd ever want. Money. Fulfillment. That's what I can offer you. So what do you say?"

"I guess to start with, I'd say I'm very flattered . . ."

"I can hear the 'but' coming," Smith good-naturedly groaned.

"Well, you're right. I'm flattered, but we really like

where we live. You know, I grew up in a big city. Big cities have their good points, I suppose. But before we were married, Leslie and I decided that we wanted to raise our children in a small town. Frank, I make as much money as I need. And I'm happy. And my family's happy. What more could I want?"

"Sounds like you haven't been bitten by the success bug. You know, I really kind of envy you. But if you ever change your mind . . ."

"You'll be the first to know," Eric promised.

🌿

Eric rose from the desk and walked to the phone. He had information place a call for him.

"Hello," a voice answered.

"Frank?"

"Yeah, who's this?"

"This is Eric Sanders. You remember the little talk we had a couple of years ago?"

"Yeah," drawled Smith, a little cautiously.

"Well, is your offer still good?"

"You mean about your working for me?" Smith suddenly sounded excited.

"Yeah, that's what I mean."

"Are you kidding? Of course, it's still good."

Chapter Seven

*E*ric never remarried. He was very successful at his job. He worked on the big projects and made the big money. Frank Smith retired, and Eric ended up becoming head of the firm. But there was still the empty feeling which had never completely left him. Time had dulled the pain. But there were nights—too many nights—when he'd lay awake and wonder bitterly about the so-called meaning of life. What did it all mean? What was it all for? If the people who mattered most to you could be taken in an instant, what really mattered?

He had never been back to the small town where the tragedy occurred. But more and more lately he'd had a nagging feeling that he should go back there for a visit. He knew he probably could never come to terms with the past, but at least perhaps he should face it.

It was a week before Christmas when the nagging feeling hit harder than usual. He had just wished his housekeeper a pleasant holiday season and given her a box of chocolates and an envelope with a $100 bonus in it. She was happy and excited, for she was going to spend the next two weeks in Puerto Rico visiting family and friends. After she left, Eric wondered how he should spend the holidays.

For all official purposes, Eric's firm was closed between Christmas and New Year's. Except for a few die-hard workaholics, no one would be at the office. For lack of anything better to do, Eric customarily went to work and reprimanded those he found there for not being home and enjoying the holidays. For those he failed to chase home, Eric would send out for pizza or deli food.

Maybe now would be a good time to go back, thought Eric. *There's really nothing to do at work. I could go to the Christmas program. I've got to go back sometime, and maybe this would be as good a time as any. I could stay at the bed and breakfast. I wonder if Mrs. Heath still runs it?*

The bed and breakfast was a fine old house with gingerbread trim. And during the holidays, Mrs. Heath could always be counted on to make her famous cranberry walnut muffins and warm spiced apple cider.

Eric got the number for the bed and breakfast from information and after a friendly voice said hello, he asked for Mrs. Heath.

"I'm sorry, but Mrs. Heath passed away four years ago. I'm Natalie Sorenson. I've been running the place for the past three years."

"My name's Eric Sanders, and I'd like to see if I could arrange to stay at your place for about ten days starting on the twenty-second."

"Would it be just you?"

"Yes."

"Well, let me check my book here . . . Yes, I've got a single room you could have."

Chapter Eight

*M*rs. Sorenson was a pleasant woman in her sixties. Eric's first morning there he breakfasted on ripe cantaloupe and blueberry pancakes.

"Your pancakes were just great, Mrs. Sorenson. But I've just got to ask you about your cantaloupe. You see, when I was growing up, I took ripe cantaloupes for granted. My mom possessed a real knack for picking out sweet, ripe cantaloupes—a talent which I unfortunately didn't inherit. I thump 'em and squeeze 'em; I even feel the texture of their skin—that's what a doctor friend of mine told me to do—and I still end up with cantaloupes that are crunchy and taste like cardboard. So after tasting this perfect cantaloupe, I've got to ask you: what's your secret? What method do you use?"

Mrs. Sorenson smiled and said, "I hate to disappoint you, Mr. Sanders, but I haven't got any system. We just happen to have a really good produce man here in town, and he won't put anything out for sale unless it's just right."

"Well, then, I'm simply going to have to come here to buy my cantaloupes."

As they continued to chat, Eric learned that Mrs. Sorenson was a widow, that her husband had been an insurance executive. "Ed had a bad heart, and I got him to retire early. I tried to get him to slow down, but something about living in the city made it impossible for him to relax. He'd go to basketball games and come home upset over the traffic and parking.

"So I convinced him that we should move to a smaller town. And I always thought that running a bed and breakfast would be fun. I told our real estate agent to find us a bed and breakfast. And she found us this. Ed and I had a wonderful year together. He enjoyed puttering around the place playing fix-up man. And there were some retired fellows that actually got Ed to take up fishing. But then his heart finally gave out on him. The kids wanted me to move closer to them, but I decided to stay here because this just feels like home. It's like I've always lived here."

"You know, that's how it felt for me when I lived here," said Eric.

"I take it you've been gone a long time?"

"Yeah, it's been years."

"So why exactly did you move?"

Eric visibly stiffened. "Oh . . . I was offered a job in the city." Eric looked at his watch. "You know, I guess I'd better be off. I'm just going to leave my car here and walk—just walk around and absorb the sights and sounds. And it'll be interesting to see how much the town has changed."

The only thing constant is change. The familiar old adage—an oft-quoted favorite of one of Eric's high school English teachers—came to mind and seemed particularly apt as he walked through the town. Mrs. Tate's Homemade Candies was now a dress shop, and Kessler's Office Supply had been converted to a beauty salon.

But the old café was still there. The name was different, but it looked pretty much the same. Eric went in and found that the menu still featured staples of the American diet: burgers, fries, shakes. He was looking out the window at some kids playing in the snow when he noticed someone slide into the facing seat in his booth.

"Eric, is that you?" asked a middle-aged man.

It was Brent Watkins. Brent was Eric's age. They had

played golf together. Eric was startled to see Brent with greying hair and lines well on their way to becoming wrinkles around his eyes and mouth. *Do I look that old?* Eric wondered.

There was a palpable tension between them as they made amiable small talk.

"You remember Lenny, the guy that used to run this place?" asked Brent.

Eric nodded.

"You know how he was always talking about going back to school. Well, one day he finally did. Up and moved his family. I saw him a couple of years ago. Know what he does? He's a full-fledged college professor. Teaches history, or something like that. You know, I just can't imagine him doing anything besides flipping burgers. Have you been back to town at all?"

"No."

"Then I guess you wouldn't know. But since Lenny left, this café's been Chinese, Mexican and Italian. There was even a guy threatening to turn it into a sushi bar—but the backing fell through. And now it's back to burgers and shakes."

"Full circle," said Eric.

"Yeah, full circle." Brent looked awkwardly down at his hands. He'd run out of small talk. Yet there was still something he wanted to say. He let out a slow breath, then said, "You know, Eric, I'm really glad I ran into you. I didn't sit down here just to chit chat with you. There's something I've wanted to tell you for a lot of years. And since we're friends, I feel like I can talk to you.

"After the accident, well, it's like you just disappeared. . . . One day you were just gone, and no one seemed to know where you went. But there's something I want to tell you—about how the accident affected me.

"You know I'm no philosopher, and—like you—I'm not what you'd call religious. And I don't pretend to know why God—if there is one— would *let* something like that happen.

"And when I saw you just now, I wasn't sure if it would be appropriate to tell you how I felt or not. But then I put myself in your place. And I thought if it were me, if that had happened to my family, I'd want to know if there was anything, anything at all, that was the least bit—'positive' really isn't the right word—but I guess if there was anything the least bit meaningful or worthwhile that had come out of such a terrible thing. Well, all I know, is that it was such a senseless thing—that if it were me, I'd want to know if anything came from it that made any kind of sense at all.

"You see, Eric, because I knew you so well and your kids, I was really shaken up. This was the kind of thing you'd hear about on the news and shake your head and say 'Too bad.' But then this happened, and it was *here* and I *knew* the people. And I knew that if it could happen this close, it could have happened to me—it could have been *my* family.

"And because this is a small town, I think a lot of people felt the way I did.

"But all I know, is that accident really made me take stock of my life. And I realized that I'd been taking my family for granted. And from that time on, whenever I felt myself getting cross with the kids or about to be sharp with my wife, I'd think about the accident—and I'd know that all of them could be taken away from me forever in an instant. For whatever it's worth, that awful tragedy made me a better father and husband. And I think a lot of parents were kinder to their children, and held them in their arms more after the accident.

"You know, Eric, I'm not suggesting that you should

get any comfort out of hearing this. But like I say, for whatever it's worth, I thought you might want to know that in a really significant way—significant at least to me and my family—there was something worthwhile that came out of that tragedy."

A moment passed between them in silence. Then Eric cleared his throat and said softly, "I appreciate you telling me that, Brent."

🌿

When Eric left the diner, the setting sun was casting a salmon-pink glow upon the snow. He walked slowly down Main Street. Mendelsohn's Hardware was now a computer store. . . .

Chapter Nine

*F*or as long as anyone could remember, there had always been a town Christmas program the night before Christmas Eve. Eric had learned from Mrs. Sorenson that there still was a Christmas program, but he wondered if the format was still the same. The program was always conducted by a community leader—usually the mayor, but occasionally a police chief or judge. There would always be a message from a local religious leader. And then members of the audience were invited to the podium to share their memories of past Christmases or thoughts about the present holiday season. And, of course, there would always be a few numbers sung by a community or high school choir.

Eric arrived early and sat up front. Being here triggered a lot of memories of other Christmas programs. He remembered when Ned Matheson, the town bachelor, went to the pulpit, said a few words about Christmas, then abruptly proposed to Anne Nebeker, the third-grade school teacher. She promptly fainted, the whole meeting was in an uproar, and Ned was looking confused and guilty for causing it all.

"Can I sit by you, mister?"

Eric turned to find a young boy with wrinkled clothes and unruly hair smiling at him.

"Sure, son. Where's your mom and dad?"

"Mom's working. She's a bartender. And Dad, well . . . he doesn't come to stuff like this. I'm Kenny. What's your name, mister?"

"I'm Eric. Eric Sanders. It looks like they're getting ready to start."

The mayor welcomed everybody and said a few words about Christmas. He then introduced the main speaker for the evening, a Bishop Lundeval.

Kenny whispered, "He's the bishop where I go to church. My mom and dad don't go to any church. But I go with my friend and his family. When it's okay with my mom and dad, they pick me up and take me to their church. I like going to church with my friend. His family's real nice. Do you go to church?"

"No, I don't. But it's good that you do. I did when I was

your age. But then I got busy and got out of the habit. But I hope you keep going to church."

"Oh, I intend to. Our teacher gives us treats if we're good," Kenny said enthusiastically.

The bishop was a kind-looking man with wavy silver hair. He spoke about finding the true meaning of Christmas, and in closing made reference to Longfellow's "I Heard the Bells on Christmas Morn."

"Here we have a man," said the bishop, "who is cynical and discouraged. He hears the Christmas bells and reacts negatively. Let me read a few lines for you:

Then in despair I bowed my head:
"There is no peace on earth," I said
"For hate is strong and mocks the song,
Of peace on earth, goodwill to men."

"But the important thing is that he doesn't give up. He keeps listening to the bells. Let's read what happens:

Then pealed the bells more loud and deep:
"God is not dead, nor doth he sleep;
The wrong shall fail, the right prevail,
With peace on earth, goodwill to men."

"We should all be like the person in the poem. He had

almost given up on mankind. But then he listened to the Christmas bells and found new hope.

"Now, I've always loved the sound of Christmas bells and what they represent. And tonight, I feel particularly inspired to offer a suggestion. Tonight when you hear the Christmas bells, listen, really *listen.* Not just with your ears, but with your heart and soul. Listen to the Christmas bells, and see if you can hear a special message just for you."

The bishop concluded his talk and the mayor was again at the podium.

"Thank you, Bishop Lundeval, for a most inspiring message. Now we're going to have a musical number. For those of you that don't know, Mr. Starley is the high school music teacher here. And this year, he has a special treat for us. He's written a new song called 'The Spirit of Christmas.'"

Mr. Starley was a young man wearing a brightly colored sweater. He sat at the piano and began singing in a tentative baritone.

"Taking time to visit old friends,
And taking the time to be with your loved ones.
Feeling warm inside each time the carols start.

This is the Spirit of Christmas.
Sharing the Spirit of Christmas
Brings peace and joy to every heart."

As Mr. Starley sang the second verse, he gained a little more confidence and his voice became more earnest.

"Telling tales about old Saint Nick
And singing about the babe in the manger.
Feeling close to friends, although you're far apart.
This is the Spirit of Christmas.
Sharing the Spirit of Christmas
Brings peace and joy to every heart."

Then the high school choir rose and sang with Mr. Starley as the song neared its conclusion.

It was the same ragtag collection of small town kids that Eric remembered listening to at Christmas programs in years past. The group was a jumble of braces and acne and self-consciousness. There was the football player: large and sullen—obviously not there by choice but merely fulfilling a requirement. There was the timid girl with long straight hair and the popular boy with the winning smile. There was the class clown and the farm boy, sleepy from rising at dawn to milk the cows.

The individuals changed, but the collective character and makeup of the group remained constant. And Eric found comfort in this singular manifestation of constancy. For Eric, the unpolished voices of the choir sounded true and clear.

"Peace on earth,
And goodwill to all,
That's the old familiar phrase,
That we sing as we celebrate
This wondrous day of days."

Near the end of the song, the football player's eyes no longer reflected resentment. Somehow catching the spirit of the music, even he was haltingly singing from his heart.

After the song, the mayor invited members of the audience to share their feelings about Christmas. The mayor's wife recounted a Christmas she celebrated while visiting Sweden. An elderly man elaborated on the theme of the bishop's talk. He spoke in patriarchal fashion, occasionally raising his cane to emphasize a point. A few children got up and made their Christmas wants and needs known just in case Santa or one of his elves was listening.

Then a woman rose and walked to the podium. She

struck Eric as vaguely familiar. She was lanky yet elegant. She wore a flowing gown of rust and gold. She was urbane, sophisticated—yet there was a down-to-earth part imbedded in her persona—a simple, charming quality in her character—that persistently kept shining through.

Somehow Eric felt that he knew her. Could it possibly be Ellen Michelsen, the girl who used to babysit for them? But no; he recognized this woman from the newspapers or magazines. But who was she? He finally realized it was the celebrated portrait artist Ellen Evans. And he remembered that he had seen her picture in the newspaper with a story about how she had just finished painting a portrait of the president. But wait, that couldn't be. This woman was clearly Ellen Michelsen just grown up. Grown up. *Of course!* Eric suddenly felt stupid. *Evans* was obviously Ellen Michelsen's married name.

"I really shouldn't be here," she began. "A gallery in New York is opening a show of my paintings tonight, and I sort of promised I'd be there. But out of the blue I decided it was time our family had an old-fashioned Christmas—and here we are. I haven't been back here in years, but I grew up here. You might remember a girl named Ellen

Michelsen. Well, that's me, only now I'm Ellen Evans.

"Since I was a little girl, I wanted to paint. When I became a teenager, I went through some real difficult times. I was the tallest girl in school. I felt like I was the tallest girl in the universe. I felt so awkward and unaccepted. I withdrew into my art. I had this romantic notion of my lot being that of the suffering artist. You know, like if van Gogh was a lonely social outcast, I should be, too.

"So this meant being friendless and not participating in anything fun or social. I was this way until my senior year. But as my senior year began, I started thinking about changing my life, about having some fun and joining in with others.

"And again—another romantic notion!—I thought that rejoining the human race meant giving up my art. So I stopped painting, which made me miserable, and I made a few clumsy attempts to make some friends. But I guess people still thought of me as the creative outcast. I wanted to tell them, 'Look, I'm not an artist anymore. I've given it up. I'm one of you now.'

"So there I was, still friendless—only now I didn't even have my art to find comfort in. Part of me said, 'To heck with people; I'll just withdraw back into my art.' But then there was another part in me that wanted to keep trying to connect with people.

"When the holidays came I was really depressed. But I'll never forget that wonderful Christmas morning. There on the porch was the most beautiful easel in the world. It was made of solid honey-colored oak. And as the morning sun hit it, it glistened like gold.

"I couldn't believe my eyes. And I couldn't believe that someone thought enough of me to give me such a wonderful present. I remember I couldn't wait to try it out. I forgot all about my dramatic resolution to give up art. I spent the majority of Christmas day happily painting.

"And something really wonderful and strange happened. At the time, I didn't really notice what was happening. In school I became involved in painting scenery for the school play. And I was asked to draw the cover for the yearbook. Gradually, I became a happy person. Happy in my art, and happy with people. I think the reason for this was because I was becoming comfortable with myself. I was an artist, I would always be an artist— but I didn't have to withdraw from the human race. And it was like a revelation to me that becoming involved with others didn't mean having to abandon my art.

"And I know what you're thinking. All this because of an easel? And all I can say is that the easel came at a cross-roads in my life. And it helped me to think that somebody out there must have thought I was pretty special.

"I've always wondered who it was that gave me that easel. But I've never figured it out. And it's too bad, because I'd like to tell that person just what that special gift has meant to me. I still paint on that easel. The wood is still strong. And I hope to use it for years to come. I guess it's kind of my good luck charm."

Ellen Evans spoke a few more minutes, then concluded and went back to her seat.

A man rose from the back of the hall. He was a big man who walked with a powerful, lumbering gait. He had bright blond hair, and biceps that bulged the sleeves of his expensive looking suit. The crowd began to buzz with excitement. Kenny nudged Eric and whispered, "Hey mister, that's Lucky Anderson, the baseball player."

Eric knew of Lucky Anderson, the golden boy of base-ball, the player who could virtually do no wrong. Eric wondered what someone of Lucky Anderson's stature would be doing here in town. As Lucky stood behind the pulpit, Eric studied his face.

No, it can't be, thought Eric. *But it is. That's little Chet Anderson, all grown up.* Eric had watched countless games in which Lucky Anderson played a key role. But he had never before made the connection between Lucky Anderson, the celebrity athlete, and little Chet Anderson, the waif-like kid he had felt so sorry for.

"You know," Lucky began, "right now I'm supposed to be at a Christmas party being thrown by our team owner. But like Ellen, I just felt like I should be here for Christmas. I can't explain it, but that's how it is.

"You know, this town has a lot of memories for me. And, to be honest, not all of them are good.

"It's kinda weird. They call me Lucky nowadays. But growing up, that was the one thing I wasn't.

"When you grow up the son of the town drunk, you learn to try and ignore the whispers behind your back and the sad looks you'd get from people. But my mom was a proud woman. She held her head up high, and if you didn't know better you'd never imagine that she was the wife of the town drunk. I was once with her when she had to go to the old man's boss asking to let him have his job back. I knew she must have been dying inside. But she didn't beg or plead. That wasn't her style. She kept her dignity and calmly assured the man that her husband would show up for work on time and sober and that all he needed was another chance. And even when there was a bruise on her face, my mom never flinched in public. But at home it was a different story. I can remember coming home from school, and there'd be my mom, just crying in the front room.

"A couple of older kids at school made sure I was aware that my old man had a girlfriend over in Sommerville. I didn't believe it at first. But when I saw how bad he treated my mom, I knew it must be true.

"One night I heard him come home, and he started in on Mom. I remember flinching each time he hit her. Finally things settled down, but I didn't sleep that night. And I made a vow that he would never lay a hand on my mother again.

"Well, it wasn't more than a couple of weeks later that I woke up one night and heard my dad yelling and my mother starting to cry. I ran out into the front room and yelled, 'Dad, don't do it.' He told me to go back to bed, but I just stood there. Even though he was drunk, I think he could see in my eyes that I meant business. 'You want to take me on?' he said. 'No,' I said, 'but I'm not going to let you hit Mom anymore.' He looked at me and kind of sneered, then he slapped Mom hard. It's hard to describe what happened next. But it's like I had a power surge through my body.

"He fought me with the strength he would have fought another man. And I fought him with the strength of a man. I kept knocking him down, and he kept coming at me with a look like he couldn't believe what was happening. And I'd knock him down again. And each time he got up a little slower. And then finally he didn't get up.

"The next day Dad was real quiet—apologetic-like and humble. But I knew that we weren't a family anymore. And that afternoon he left, and Mom and I both knew he was never coming back. I later heard that he was living with the woman in Sommerville.

"When he was gone, it was peaceful . . . it was *definitely* peaceful . . . but it was also—this might be hard for you to understand—but it was also kind of lonely. So far, all I've told you guys about is how rotten my old man was. But, you know, there was a decent side to him. When my old man was sober, there was nobody finer or more fun to be around. My old man invented games—games that didn't need expensive equipment. I mean, who needed a ball when you could play catch with a chunk of old tire? And we had our own version of basketball. From twenty feet, we chucked empty cans into the garbage can. So what I'm trying to say is that in a lot of ways—well, really in most ways—it was good that he left—but we still missed him, too.

"You know, we have a team psychologist that pumps us up mentally. He talks a lot about having confidence and good self-esteem. Well, I think about myself growing up, and I realize that I had absolutely no self-esteem. And I remember, the holidays were coming, and it was going to be our first Christmas without Dad. I was really blue. You see, I used to just be the son of the town drunk. Now I was the son of the town drunk who had deserted his family. And I felt like it was my fault that Dad had left.

"And I knew there wasn't going to be much of a Christmas. We'd never really had much for Christmas, but this year was going to be leaner than ever. And I remember going over to Mr. Mendelsohn's Hardware Store and looking over all the toys, and then just feeling sorry for myself.

"I remember I got up Christmas morning, and opened the front door to let the dog out. And there was something on the doorstep. I ripped off the paper and there was a beautiful baseball glove. I remember that wonderful smell of the new leather. It was a tad big for me, but it didn't matter. Now I could play ball with the other kids. And on that Christmas day, I played catch with the neighbor boy. I used my new glove to catch the snowballs he pitched to me.

"You know, when I first started playing in the minors, I got the nickname Lucky because it seemed like I was always catching the ball just when our team needed it most. The nickname stuck. But let me let you in on a little secret. It was the glove that did it for me. You see, I'm still using that glove. Oh, I've had it restitched, and some of the leather's had to be replaced. But it's the same old glove.

"You see, I'd had that glove maybe three or four years when I noticed the darndest thing. It was like the glove pulled my hand up to catch the ball. Now I know that our team psychologist would have some fancy explanation that it's all in my subconscious and that the glove really isn't magic. But for me—it's magic.

"I've taken up too much of your time, but I guess my point is that, like Ellen there, my most special Christmas took place here in this town. You know, I'm good at playing ball, but I'm lousy with words. I can't really put into words what's in my heart, except to say I feel like I've been really blessed, and I love all of you here. And I hope you all have a merry Christmas."

Eric watched Lucky make his way back to his seat. One brave boy approached him for his autograph. When Lucky signed it, another boy became emboldened and approached him with a similar request.

"Now folks," the mayor was at the podium, "I'm sure Lucky didn't come here to sign autographs. I'm sure he'll be glad to visit with you later, but right now let's let him enjoy the rest of the program." The mayor had spoken with the officious yet nonthreatening voice he found effective in city business meetings. The voice proved just as effective in the present informal setting: After signing an autograph for the second boy, Lucky proceeded to his seat unhindered.

Another man was now at the podium. Being bald made him look older than he really was.

"That's Mr. Riley," whispered Kenny. He was really enjoying his role of dispensing information to Eric; it made him feel grown up and important. "Mr. Riley works at the store in the part where they sell fruits and vegetables."

"I'll have to thank him for the cantaloupe," quipped Eric. The comment bewildered Kenny, but Eric didn't explain any further. He was concentrating on the face of Mr. Riley. In his mind, Eric added some hair and took off a few pounds and years.

Of course, little Howie Riley. The son of the office cleaners.

"I feel a little funny following such inspiring stories," Riley began. "I wish I could say that I had a Christmas that inspired me to go on and do great things, like the stories we've just heard.

"To Lucky and Ellen,"—Riley looked directly at them— "I'd just like to say thank you for sharing your stories with us. You probably don't remember me, but I remember you guys growing up. I've followed Lucky's career. And I've got a print of one of Ellen's paintings in my front room. My name's Howard Riley—well, back then they called me Howie. I'm the produce manager at the store here.

"I hesitated coming up here because the stories so far have been so inspiring, and I'm afraid that my story really isn't much to hear. But I still want to share it with you.

"I had something special happen to me when I was nine or ten. And it was the same type of thing that happened to Ellen and Lucky. Someone had left a gift on our porch. And I can still see it now: bright red wrapping paper and a white satin bow. I opened it up, and I couldn't believe it. It was a train set. It was just what I had wanted, only I knew our family couldn't afford one.

"I enjoyed that set for years—making the tracks in circles and figure eights, and making mountains out of stacked books.

"I've always wondered who it was that gave me that train set. If I ever found out, I'd love to tell that person how much enjoyment I got from that gift.

"That's really all I've got to say. And I just hope you all have a happy holiday season."

A few others spoke and then suddenly Eric found himself on his feet heading for the podium. His heart was pounding, and he had no idea of what to say.

"Some of you might remember me. I used to live here. I see some familiar faces. But mostly new faces. Most of you were still children when I left here. I really don't know how to put what I feel into words. But you'll never know what coming here and listening to all of you—and this beautiful music—and—and I just want to thank all of you for making this night so special for me."

Chapter Ten

*W*hile the high school choir and audience sang some final carols together, Eric tried to take in all that had just happened. Those gifts from the attic—he hadn't thought about those gifts in years. And, incredibly, they had accomplished what he had originally intended for them to do. The glove had worked its magic and accompanied its owner to more than one World Series. The easel had helped rekindle an interest in art. And the train set . . . *Well, it didn't actually inspire anyone to build a train,* thought Eric, wryly, *but it did make a young person happy.*

The singing ended, a benediction was offered, and people began filtering out the doors. Kenny's voice pulled Eric from his reverie. "Well, mister, uh . . . what was your name again, mister?"

"It's Sanders."

"Well, Mr. Sanders, thanks for letting me sit with you. Guess I'll walk home."

"You're not walking home by yourself, are you?"

"Well—yeah."

"Not anymore you're not. Let me walk you home, my friend."

As they made their way to the exit, a lot of townspeople rushed up to Eric with hugs and handshakes. While some people were hazily familiar to him, Eric was embarrassed at the number of people he didn't remember. But the warm feelings associated with life in a small, closely-knit community—*that* he remembered.

Outside, the night air was invigorating. Kenny cheerfully chattered away, pointing out landmarks and indicating where his schoolmates lived.

They had been walking for several blocks when they approached a house with a wrought iron fence. There was something a little out of the ordinary beyond the fence. Eric blinked hard.

"Is that what I think it is?" Even though it was dark, there was enough glow from the moon that he could make out a familiar dark shape silhouetted against the snow.

"Sure," said Kenny, "It's a train. Mr. Riley built it for all us kids."

Eric stared in disbelief at the junior-sized train. He'd seen similarly sized trains used for rides in parks and zoos.

"You can't see it 'cause of the snow," continued Kenny, "but there's a track that goes in a circle. Takes up his whole front yard. Most Saturday mornings, if he's not busy, he gives any kid who wants to a train ride."

This is truly a night of miracles, thought Eric. *Old miracles I'm just finding out about.*

"You okay?" asked Kenny.

"Yeah, I'm fine."

"Well, you looked kind of funny there for a minute."

"I'm fine. Guess we'd better keep walking—don't want to get you home too late."

"Yeah, I'm kind of getting tired."

"It's funny, I just remembered something," said Eric. "You know what I wanted to do when I was your age? I wanted to be an engineer—an engineer of a big train. Wear one of those hats, and pull on the whistle, and all that."

They walked in silence a few moments, then Eric

asked, "So tell me, Kenny, what is it *you* want to do?"

"Oh, I guess go home, have a glass of milk and go to bed."

"No, I mean when you're grown up."

"Aw, you'll laugh. My teacher did when I told her. You see, maybe you haven't noticed, but I'm not really what you'd call smart. I guess I'm really kind of stupid."

"Look," said Eric, stopping and looking directly at Kenny, "I know you don't know me. And there's no reason for you to believe what I say. But let me tell you something: You are not stupid. Most kids your age couldn't carry on a conversation with an adult like you have. And another thing: I won't laugh at you—*with* you, sure, but never *at* you. Do you understand?"

"Yeah, I guess so."

"So are you going to tell me what you want to do?"

"Yeah, I'll tell you, but I could never really do it."

"Let me tell you something: You can do anything you want to, if you really put your mind to it."

"You really think so? Well, it's like this. I really like stars. I want to be an astronomer. But my teacher says you have to know a lot of math and stuff."

"Well, Kenny. You're going to be an astronomer, if that's what you really want to be. You see, Kenny,

Christmas is a time of miracles. Believe me. I know."

"You're kind of strange . . ." Kenny said, inoffensively, then added, "I've never met anyone like you, mister."

They walked on a few moments in silence. Then Kenny said, "Well, here's where I live."

It was a small rundown house.

"Will you come in and see my Christmas tree?" Kenny asked, hopefully.

"Sure."

There was an unshaven, disheveled man wearing a grimy T-shirt half-asleep on the couch.

"My dad," Kenny said a little sheepishly. "My tree's here in the kitchen."

On the kitchen table was a plastic tree about twelve inches tall.

"I bought it with my own money, and I decorated it myself."

"It's a fine tree."

"Do you think Santa Claus will like it?"

"Of course he will."

A loud, unpleasant bellow came from the front room. Then: "Kenny!" Eric stayed in the kitchen while Kenny went to his father.

"Where have you been, you little brat!" The father's speech was slurred. He didn't notice Eric watching from the kitchen. "I asked you a question!"

"Remember, I told you, Dad. I-I went to the Christmas program."

"You little liar. You didn't tell me nothing. . . ."

"But Dad, remember, right before I left—"

"Shut up! You know somethin'—you're really good for nothin' . . . !" He stood up, staggered into the bathroom, and slammed the door. Kenny looked back at Eric.

"I'm sorry, Mr. Sanders. My dad isn't always like this."

They went out to the porch in embarrassed silence, then Eric said, "Just remember what I told you. Kenny, you can do anything you want to—if you put your mind to it. Don't worry about your dad or your mom or anybody that would make you feel like you're anything less than very special. All you do is love your mom and dad—and never forget: You're special and you have unlimited potential."

"Unlimited what-you-said . . . what does that mean?"

"It means you can do whatever you put your mind to. Now, promise you won't forget?"

Kenny looked a little uncertain, but then in a solemn voice said, "Promise."

They made some small talk for a few minutes, then wished each other a Merry Christmas and parted.

As Eric walked in the night, he was impressed by the utter stillness around him. There was no traffic. No dogs were barking. Just silence and calm. He started to hum "Silent Night." While he softly hummed, his mind raced.

He could hardly wait for tomorrow to come. He wouldn't bother looking for a telescope here; he doubted he'd find one. Instead, he'd get up early and drive to Sommerville, which had two large department stores. And if he couldn't find a telescope there he'd drive on to Centerfield. And if he couldn't find one there, he'd keep on driving until he found one. And he wouldn't get just any telescope. It would have to be special. He'd wrap the telescope in bright red paper and leave it on Kenny's porch.

Chapter Eleven

*A*s Eric approached the center of town he was still thinking about the telescope. The streets were deserted and, in the dark stillness, each step he took sounded distinctly and echoed softly. The big courthouse clock read five minutes to ten. During the Christmas season, after tolling the hour, the big clock's bells played carols. Eric decided to wait for the bells. As he stood in the empty square with stray snowflakes drifting down, he tried to remember what the bishop had said earlier tonight about Christmas bells.

Tonight, when you hear the Christmas bells, I want you to listen. Really listen with your whole heart and soul. And see if you can find a special message in them for you.

The bells began chiming: first the steady ringing marking the time and then a sweet Christmas medley. Eric listened. He listened with his whole soul. *Now what was that?* There *was* something. Something more than the bells. Some new sound. And he was hearing it not with his ears but with his heart. A voice, no *voices.* Distant, yet clear. And *familiar.* They were speaking together. Now if he could just make out the words. The voices weren't really speaking, nor were they singing. There was a quality to the voices that he had never heard before. The one thing he could perceive was a soothing, rhythmic quality to the voices. The voices were becoming stronger—not really louder, but more piercing. And he could now make out the words.

We're all right.
We love you.
We're all right.
We'll be together again.
We're all right.

And then two voices:

We love you, Dad.

And then one voice:

I love you, Eric.

And then the voices were gone. And the bells stopped ringing. Their silver echo hung in the air a few moments, and then a silence settled in that was profound.

As he wiped the tears from his eyes, Eric wondered why he had never heard the voices before. And then he realized he had never really tried to listen before. Not with his heart. Until he heard the bishop's talk tonight, it never really occurred to him that there was any way of listening other than with your ears. *How long have their voices been trying to reach me?* he wondered.

No matter. The important thing was that he had finally heard the voices. And for the rest of his life he would be secure in the knowledge that death was not an ending but a transition.

He *would* see his family again.

And they *were* all right.

Chapter Twelve

*C*hristmas came. And with it came the sounds of wrapping paper being hastily ripped and wadded, youthful squeals of delight, and the happy cacophony of growling space monsters, talking dolls, rockets and roller skates and racing cars. New violins and trumpets and drums were exuberantly (if not expertly) played. And the familiar smells of roast turkeys, and baked hams, and sweet spices mingled with the tangy scent of Christmas trees.

On Christmas night, the air was crisp and the sky was clear. Many out-of-town visitors reluctantly drove back home. Some families gathered around the fireside, while others were busily making order out of the chaos of crumpled wrapping paper and scattered toys. A few industrious souls cheerfully toiled in kitchens where mounds of silverware and piles of dishes bore silent witness of tremendous feasts. Some children and many grownups, exhausted from the frenzy of the day's activity, slept soundly. And with his new telescope, a young boy gazed in wonder at the stars, while a man, hidden behind some nearby bushes, contentedly looked upon the boy.

Afterword:

The Inspiration for
Christmas Gifts, Christmas Voices

❦

everal years ago I was offered a twelve-month contract to work on a writing project. One condition of the contract was that it would require temporarily relocating to a small rural town. After discussing the matter with my family, we decided to accept the contract and make the move.

Shortly after our move, we made the acquaintance of a wonderful family. In this family there were two teenage brothers. These boys were fun-loving, industrious, and active in scouting, school and their church. They both had a particular love for music.

One Sunday morning, about a week before Christmas, they and two young women were driving to a nearby town to perform a vocal number at a church meeting. The road to the church ran parallel to a deep river. It was a sunny morning and the road was free of snow. However, coming upon a portion of road that was in the shade, they hit an unexpected icy patch and skidded into the river. All four occupants of the car were drowned.

When I heard the news I was devastated. My personally having known the brothers made it all the harder for me: They exemplified all that is right with youth.

At the time I had three daughters (I now have four), and I kept thinking about how the parents must feel. I imagined them casually bidding their children farewell, with no reason not to expect them home by lunchtime. I imagined them hearing the awful, surrealistic news— the news too terrible to be true.

You hear about tragedies, you shake your head and mutter "Too bad," and then go on with your life. You accept the fact that tragedies happen in life—but they happen to other people, not you. And then there is the tragedy that affects someone you know, someone close to you, and you realize that that individual—just like you—thought terrible tragedies happened only to "the other person." And that's when you acknowledge the possibility that in an instant you can become "the other person": Your life can be changed forever by a horrendous tragedy.

The night of the terrible accident I tried to make a

bargain with God. I said I would gladly pass through any trials associated with Earth life if He could just guarantee one thing—the safety and health of my children. I received the strong impression that I, a mere mortal, was in no position to set the terms of a divine bargain. It was hard for me to accept that I couldn't frame some kind of agreement that would absolutely guarantee the safety of my children.

The next day, my wife and I visited the parents of the boys who drowned. Any words I could say seemed inadequate and hollow. All I could do was wrap the father in a bear hug and cry with him. The last thing my friends ever thought would happen would be the loss of a child—let alone the loss of two children. And yet it happened. And if it happened to them, it could happen to me and my wife.

I finally came to terms with the fact that you can lose anybody anytime. That's just one of the perils of Earth life. The conclusion I reached is expressed in my book by the minor character Brent Watkins.

Concerning the book's climax, I have never personally experienced anything like Eric Sanders' miracle. But I have known honest, serious-minded people—people grounded in reality, not given to flights of fancy—who have. For some reason (I have never solicited nor would I ever solicit such information), these people have felt comfortable enough in the course of a conversation to share their other-worldly experiences with me in soberness and sincerity. Why some experience the miracle and others do not is open to speculation. I think it may have something to do with the unique economy of heaven and perhaps the situation specific to each person.

One final thought concerning the attic gifts. Throughout my life I have been impressed by the "ripple effect"—how just like the stone thrown in a pond creates ever-widening ripples, so can our actions have far-reaching consequences often unknown to us. I think we do more good than we know. And if we're aware of the ripple effect, hopefully we'll keep striving to do good.

—John Allen

Ordinary people can make an extraordinary difference!

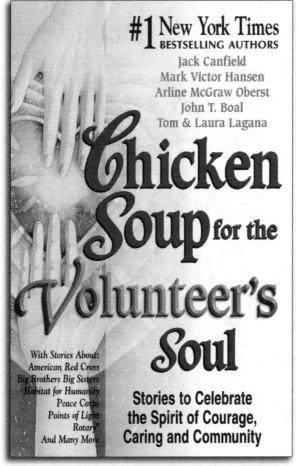

#1 New York Times
BESTSELLING AUTHORS
Jack Canfield
Mark Victor Hansen
Arline McGraw Oberst
John T. Boal
Tom & Laura Lagana

Chicken Soup for the *Volunteer's Soul*

With Stories About:
American Red Cross
Big Brothers Big Sisters
Habitat for Humanity
Peace Corps
Points of Light
Rotary®
And Many More

Stories to Celebrate the Spirit of Courage, Caring and Community

Code #0146 • Paperback • $12.95

This heartfelt collection captures the defining moments of true kindness and will inspire you to greater personal growth and spiritual awareness.

A Timeless Holiday Collection

#1 New York Times
BESTSELLING AUTHORS

Jack Canfield
Mark Victor Hansen

Chicken Soup for the Soul® Christmas Treasury

Holiday Stories to Warm the Heart

Code #0006 • Special Hardcover Edition • $16.95

The stories in *Chicken Soup for the Soul Christmas Treasury* will fill your heart with the profound joy that Christmas brings. Share this special holiday keepsake with those you love.

Celebrate the Holidays

Jack Canfield
Mark Victor Hansen
Patty Hansen
Irene Dunlap

Chicken Soup for the Soul® Christmas Treasury for Kids

A Story a Day from December 1st
Through Christmas for
Kids and Their Families

Code #0383 • Special Hardcover Edition • $14.95

Celebrating the holidays will be a special treat with *Chicken Soup for the Soul Christmas Treasury for Kids.*

Pure Inspiration

#1 New York Times
BESTSELLING AUTHORS
Jack Canfield
Mark Victor Hansen
Patty Aubery
Nancy Mitchell Autio
LeAnn Thieman

Chicken Soup for the *Christian Woman's Soul*

Stories to Open the Heart and Rekindle the Spirit

Code #0189 • Paperback • $12.95

#1 New York Times
BESTSELLING AUTHORS
Jack Canfield
Mark Victor Hansen
Patty & Nancy Mitchell
Heather & Katy McNamara

Chicken Soup for the *Sister's Soul*

Stories of Love and Inspiration of Sisters Across the Generations

Code #0243 • Paperback • $12.95

Enjoy these books by yourself or share them with friends and family. They will warm your heart, strengthen your spirit and improve your outlook on life.

411 for Life

Code #942X • Paperback • $12.95

Code #0227 • Paperback • $12.95

Let's face it—the pressures of life can be overwhelming. Now, *Chicken Soup* tackles some of your biggest and most challenging issues.

Also Available

Chicken Soup for the Baseball Fan's Soul
Chicken Soup for the Canadian Soul
Chicken Soup for the Cat & Dog Lover's Soul
Chicken Soup for the Christian Family Soul
Chicken Soup for the Christian Soul
Chicken Soup for the Christian Woman's Soul
Chicken Soup for the College Soul
Chicken Soup for the Country Soul
Chicken Soup for the Couple's Soul
Chicken Soup for the Expectant Mother's Soul
Chicken Soup for the Father's Soul
Chicken Soup for the Gardener's Soul
Chicken Soup for the Golden Soul
Chicken Soup for the Golfer's Soul, Vol. I, II
Chicken Soup for the Grandparent's Soul
Chicken Soup for the Jewish Soul
Chicken Soup for the Kid's Soul
Chicken Soup for the Little Souls
Chicken Soup for the Mother's Soul, Vol. I, II
Chicken Soup for the Nurse's Soul
Chicken Soup for the Parent's Soul
Chicken Soup for the Pet Lover's Soul
Chicken Soup for the Preteen Soul
Chicken Soup for the Prisoner's Soul
Chicken Soup for the Single's Soul
Chicken Soup for the Sister's Soul
Chicken Soup for the Soul, Vol. I-VI
Chicken Soup for the Soul of America
Chicken Soup for the Soul at Work
Chicken Soup for the Soul Cookbook
Chicken Soup for the Soul Christmas Treasury, hardcover
Chicken Soup for the Soul Christmas Treasury for Kids, hardcover
Chicken Soup for the Soul Personal Journal, hardcover
Chicken Soup for the Sports Fan's Soul
Chicken Soup for the Surviving Soul
Chicken Soup for the Teacher's Soul
Chicken Soup for the Teenage Soul, Vol. I, II, III
Chicken Soup for the Teenage Soul Journal
Chicken Soup for the Teenage Soul Letters
Chicken Soup for the Teenage Soul on Love & Friendship
Chicken Soup for the Teenage Soul on Tough Stuff
Chicken Soup for the Traveler's Soul
Chicken Soup for the Unsinkable Soul
Chicken Soup for the Veteran's Soul
Chicken Soup for the Volunteer's Soul
Chicken Soup for the Woman's Soul, Vol. I, II
Chicken Soup for the Writer's Soul
Condensed Chicken Soup for the Soul
Cup of Chicken Soup for the Soul

Selected titles available in Spanish, hardcover and audio format.